Dynamic Programming by Python Examples

X.Y. Wang, Ph.D

Contents

Chapter 1

Introduction to Dynamic Programming

Dynamic Programming (DP), a term steeped in the annals of mathematical and computational history, is a technique that has fundamentally altered our approach to problem-solving. Rooted in the concept of breaking complex problems down into simpler, manageable subproblems, dynamic programming offers a means to tackle computational challenges that may appear daunting at first glance. This chapter presents an introduction to dynamic programming, illuminating its principles, historical context, and reasons for its importance in our computational toolbox.

The Genesis of Dynamic Programming

Our journey commences with the birth of dynamic programming, a term coined by the applied mathematician Richard Bellman in the 1950s. Originally, dynamic programming was conceived as a mathematical method for optimal decision-making in multistage processes, hence the term "programming" in its name. Over the subsequent decades, it has found applications in diverse disciplines such as artificial intelligence, operations research, bioinformatics, economics, and, most importantly, in computer science where it has emerged as a key algorithmic technique.

Bellman's Principle of Optimality

Central to the philosophy of dynamic programming is the Principle of Optimality, a concept eloquently first formulated by Bellman. It postulates that an optimal sequence of decisions harbors the characteristic that, irrespective of the initial state and decision, the remaining decisions must form an optimal sequence relative to the state brought about by the first decision. This optimal substructure property is the bedrock on which dynamic programming algorithms are designed and implemented.

To elucidate this principle, consider the game of chess. An optimal move at any juncture is one that will lead to a position from which the player can force a win, regardless of the opponent's subsequent moves. The optimal strategy, therefore, is composed of optimal decisions at every stage of the game.

The Rationale Behind Dynamic Programming

Dynamic programming enjoys widespread usage owing to its ability to dramatically curtail the time complexity of certain algorithms. It particularly thrives in scenarios featuring overlapping subproblems, where a given subproblem needs to be solved multiple times. Dynamic programming circumvents the issue of repeated computation by employing a strategy of memoization, storing solutions to subproblems for swift retrieval on future occasions.

The merit of dynamic programming is not confined to mere time efficiency. It also lends structure and systematicity to the problem-solving process. By providing a clear procedure for problem-solving, it demystifies the path to the solution, making it a pivotal tool for research and pedagogical purposes alike.

In this book, our endeavor is to provide an immersive exploration of dynamic programming, grounded in the firm bedrock of theory and embellished with rich examples. The objective is to instill a deep understanding of the technique, enabling the reader to apply dynamic programming to a diverse range of problems with finesse and proficiency. Let us embark on this fascinating journey into the world of dynamic programming.

Chapter 2

Understanding Recursion Through Problem Solving

2.1 Calculating Factorial Recursively

The problem at hand is to calculate factorial of a non-negative integer, using dynamic programming. The factorial of any non-negative integer n, denoted as n!, is the product of all positive integers less than or equal to n. For instance, the factorial of 4, i.e., 4! will be computed as: 4 * 3 * 2 * 1 = 24. The factorial function can be defined recursively because the factorial of a number can be defined in terms of the factorial of a smaller number.

Here's one way to solve the problem using memoization, a concept from dynamic programming, where we store solutions of sub-problems to avoid repeated calculations later:

```python
# Define a function to calculate factorial.
def Factorial(n, dp):
    '''Function to calculate factorial of a number.

    Arguments:
    n : int : input number.
    dp : list : list to store results of subproblems.

    Returns:
    int : factorial of the input number.
    '''

    # Handle base case.
    if n == 0:
        return 1

    # If we've already solved this subproblem, return the answer.
    if dp[n] != -1:
        return dp[n]

    # Otherwise, we solve the subproblem and store the result.
    dp[n] = n * Factorial(n-1, dp)

    return dp[n]

# Create list to store results of subproblems and initialize with -1
dp = [-1 for _ in range(101)] # Let's prepare for input upto 100
print(Factorial(4, dp))
```

In this code, 'dp' is a list of size 101, initialized with -1, which is used to store the factorial of all numbers up to 100. Initially, all entries in 'dp' are -1, which indicates that we haven't computed the factorial for that index yet. When we call 'Factorial(n, dp)', we first check if 'dp[n]' is not -1. If it is not -1, this means we have already computed factorial of 'n' before, so we just return it. This is how we avoid repeated calculations. If 'dp[n]' is -1, this means we need to compute factorial of 'n' and store it in 'dp[n]'.

This is a top-down approach to dynamic programming, also known as memoization. We break down the problem into smaller subproblems (in this case, calculating factorial of smaller num-

bers) and solve them to get the final solution. By memoizing
the solutions of subproblems, we ensure that each subproblem
is solved only once, thus reducing the time complexity of our
solution.

For factorial problems, this approach reduces time complexity
from $O(n!)$ for naive recursive solution to $O(n)$ for memoized
solution.

2.2 Generating Permutations using Recursion

This is a frequently raised problem which describes
generating all possible permutations of a set of distinct
elements. Suppose we have a collection of 'n' distinct
objects, and we want to arrange them into a sequence.
The number of different sequences we can make is given
by 'n¡ (n factorial). For instance, if we have three distinct objects 'a, b, c', then they can be arranged in six
different ways: 'abc, acb, bac, bca, cab, and cba'. The
objective here is to write a Python program that can
print all these different arrangements (permutations)
of any set of distinct elements.

Here is the Python code for generating all permutations of an
array using recursion.

```
def permute(arr, l, r):
    # Base case: if left index has reached right index, entire array
        has been permuted
    if l==r:
        print(arr)
    else:
        # Recursively traverse the array from the left index
        for i in range(l, r+1):
```

```
        # Swap the current element with the first element
        arr[l], arr[i] = arr[i], arr[l]
        # Find all permutations with the first element fixed
        permute(arr, l+1, r)
        # Swap the current element back with the first element to
            maintain the order
        arr[l], arr[i] = arr[i], arr[l]
# Test the function
test_arr = ['a', 'b', 'c']
n = len(test_arr)
permute(test_arr, 0, n-1)
```

In the recursion, this code first maintains an index (let's say 'l') which is initially on the first element (or the left). For each index 'l', it swaps the element at index 'l' with each element that comes after it (including the one at 'l' itself). After swapping, it fixes the element at the 'l'-th position and recurs for the remaining part to be permuted i.e., 'l+1' to 'n'. It then backtracks by again swapping the 'l'-th element and moving to next.

This approach is a form of Depth-First Search where we try to go as deep as we can (fixing elements at every depth) till we reach the end of the array (the base case). In case of 'n=3' as in the above example, the recursion tree would look like something like this:

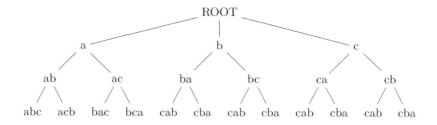

In this tree, each edge represents a swap operation. Therefore, generating permutations of an n-element sequence involves com-

plex recursive operations and the number of these operations
grows rapidly with 'n', as expected by the 'n¡ count of the permutations.

2.3   Solving Tower of Hanoi problem

**The Tower of Hanoi is a mathematical puzzle that gets
its name from the large number of disks in a small game
that was used in Hanoi. The puzzle begins with the
disks in a neat stack in ascending order of size on one
rod, the smallest at the top, making a conical shape.
The objective of the puzzle is to move the entire stack
to another rod, obeying the following simple rules:**

1. Only one disk can be moved at a time.

2. Each move consists of taking the upper disk from one of the
stacks and placing it on top of another stack or on an empty rod.

3. No disk may be placed on top of a smaller disk.

To solve the Tower of Hanoi using Dynamic Programming in
Python, we can use recursion which is a fundamental concept
in Dynamic Programming. This is the algorithm in Python:

```
def TowerOfHanoi(n , source, destination, auxiliary):
    """
    Function for TowerOfHanoi
    source: source rod to move disk from
    destination: rod to move disk to
    auxiliary: auxiliary rod used for the movements
    """

    # Base condition, if there is only one disk left, move it
        directly to the destination
    if n==1:
        print("Move disk 1 from rod",source,"to rod",destination)
        return

    # Recursive condition, for n>1
```

```
# Moving (n-1) disks from source to auxiliary rod
TowerOfHanoi(n-1, source, auxiliary, destination)
# Moving last disk from source to destination
print("Move disk",n,"from rod",source,"to rod",destination)
# Now, moving these (n-1) disks from auxiliary to destination
TowerOfHanoi(n-1, auxiliary, destination, source)

# Driver code
n = 3
# Our function for Tower Of Hanoi, we put names of rods as 'A', 'B',
    'C'
TowerOfHanoi(n,'A','B','C')
```

When we run this code for 'n=3', it prints the steps:

```
Move disk 1 from rod A to rod B
Move disk 2 from rod A to rod C
Move disk 1 from rod B to rod C
Move disk 3 from rod A to rod B
Move disk 1 from rod C to rod A
Move disk 2 from rod C to rod B
Move disk 1 from rod A to rod B
```

This is how it works:

- We move 'n-1' disks from 'A' (Source) to 'B' (Auxiliary)

- Move 'nth' disk from 'A' to 'C' (Destination)

- Now 'B' behaves as source and 'A' as auxiliary

- We again move 'n-1' disks from 'B' (Source) to 'A' (Auxiliary)

- Move 'nth' disk from 'B' to 'C'

- Finally 'A' behaves as source and 'B' as auxiliary

- We move 'n-1' disks from 'A' (Source) to 'B' (Auxiliary)

Chapter 3

Memoization and Top-Down Dynamic Programming

3.1 Memoized Fibonacci Series

The Fibonacci series is a sequence of numbers in which each number is the sum of the two preceding ones, usually starting with 0 and 1. However, we often find that in traditional recursive implementations of the Fibonacci series, there is a significant redundancy in recomputation of the same subproblems, which can drastically slow down the computation for larger input numbers.

This issue can be addressed by using Dynamic Programming,

a technique that stores the solutions of subproblems to avoid repetitive computation. In this case, a Python solution for Fibonacci series using Dynamic Programming includes using a "memoization" technique where previously calculated values are stored and retrieved when needed, instead of being recalculated.

```python
# Python program for memoized version of Fibonacci series

# function to calculate nth Fibonacci number
def fibonacci(n, lookup):

    # Base case for Fibonacci numbers
    if n == 0 or n == 1 :
        lookup[n] = n

    # If the value is not calculated previously then calculate it
    if lookup[n] is None:
        lookup[n] = fibonacci(n-1 , lookup) + fibonacci(n-2 , lookup)

    return lookup[n]

# function to initialize a lookup table
def start(n):

    # Initialize a lookup table for storing solutions to subproblems
    lookup = [None]*(n+1)
    return fibonacci(n, lookup)

# Driver program to test the functions
def main():
    n = 34
    print("Fibonacci Number is ", start(n))

# Calling main function
if __name__=="__main__":
    main()
```

In the above Python code for the Fibonacci series using Dynamic Programming, we first check if the Fibonacci result for the current 'n' is available in the 'lookup' list. If it is there, we use it directly, if it's not, we calculate it using the formula 'F(n) = F(n-1) + F(n-2)', and then store this result in 'lookup' list at the position 'n' for future reference. This process reduces the computational time drastically making it feasible to calculate the Fibonacci for large 'n' efficiently.

3.2 Longest Increasing Subsequence (Top-Down Approach)

The Longest Increasing Subsequence (LIS) problem is about finding a subsequence of a given sequence in which the subsequence's elements are in sorted order, lowest to highest, and in which the subsequence is as long as possible. This subsequence is not necessarily contiguous or unique. For example, for the sequence [10, 22, 9, 33, 21, 50, 41, 60, 80], a longest increasing subsequence is [10, 22, 33, 50, 60, 80]. The task is to find these subsequences throughout the array and calculate their lengths using dynamic programming.

Here is the Python solution for this problem:

```python
def LIS(seq):
    """ Returns the length of the longest increasing subsequence

    Args:
    seq: A list of integers

    Returns:
    An integer which represents the length of the longest increasing
        subsequence
    """
    # Initialize the lookup table with None
    lookup = [None]*len(seq)

    # Starting from the last element of the sequence
    for i in range(len(seq)-1, -1, -1): # Iterates in reversed order
        # Define the subproblem for the last element
        lookup[i] = (seq[i],) if i == len(seq)-1 else ()

        # For other elements, find the longest subsequence which
        #     starts with an element greater than seq[i]
        for j in range(i+1, len(seq)):
            # If the start of the current longest subsequence is
            #     greater than seq[i]
            if seq[i] < lookup[j][0]:
                # If the current longest subsequence plus seq[i] is
                #     longer than the current seq[i], update the
                #     subproblem
                lookup[i] = (seq[i],) + lookup[j] if len(lookup[j]) +
                    1 > len(lookup[i]) else lookup[i]
```

```
# Find the longest subsequence among the lookups
LIS = max(lookup, key=len)
return len(LIS)
```
```
# Testing
seq = [10, 22, 9, 33, 21, 50, 41, 60, 80]
print("Length of the Longest Increasing Subsequence is ", LIS(seq))
```

This Python function uses memoization to store the longest increasing subsequence that starts at each element of the sequence (from the last to the first). The function then returns the length of the longest subsequence. The function iteratively builds up the lookup table, ensuring that the solution to each subproblem is optimal, which guarantees that the end result is optimal as well. The time complexity of this approach is $O(n^2)$, where n is the length of the sequence. This dynamic programming solution therefore provides a substantial speedup over the brute force method, which would have a time complexity of $O(2^n)$.

3.3   Memoized Grid-Traveler Problem

The Grid-Traveler problem is a classic challenge in Dynamic Programming. The problem is formulated as follows: A traveler starts at the top-left corner of a 'm * n' grid (m rows and n columns) and wishes to get to the bottom-right corner. However, the traveler can only move either to the right or downwards. How many different ways can the traveler traverse finding his way through the grid?

The naive method - using recursion - for solving the problem will result in duplicated subtasks computation. This results in huge time complexity of $O(2^{m+n})$. Dynamic Programming can be employed here to optimize subtasks computation.

Here is the complete Python solution using Dynamic Programming to solve the Grid-Traveler problem using a technique called memoization to solve subproblems once and store their solutions to avoid unnecessary computations:

```python
def grid_traveler(m,n, memo=dict()):
    """
    A function to compute the number of ways to
    travel in a grid of size mXn.
    Args:
    m(int): number or rows in grid
    n(int): number or columns in grid
    memo: optional, dictionary used to store already computed
        results
    Returns:
    int: the number of ways to travel in the grid
    """

    # Key for the current subproblem in the memo
    key = str(m) + ',' + str(n)

    # Getting the stored value in memo if exists
    if key in memo: return memo[key]

    # If grid is 1X1 return 1
    if m == 1 and n == 1: return 1

    # If either rows or columns are non-positive return 0
    if m == 0 or n == 0: return 0

    # Recursive call, optimized by storing the result in a memo
        table
    # This will eliminate overlapping subproblems
    memo[key] = grid_traveler(m - 1, n, memo) + grid_traveler(m, n -
        1, memo)

    return memo[key]
```

In this code, we used a dictionary memo to store the result of each subproblem on a grid of size 'm * n', defined by the key 'm,n'. Whenever we try to solve a subproblem we check if the computed value is already in the memo. If it's found we use it and if it's not we compute it the usual way and add it to the memo for future calls.

This solution is much faster than the naive one, with a time complexity of $O(m * n)$ and a space complexity of $O(m + n)$.

Chapter 4

Tabulation and Bottom-Up Dynamic Programming

4.1 Fibonacci Series with Tabulation

Dynamic programming is essentially breaking down a complex problem into simpler subproblems, solving each subproblem just once, and storing their results in case next time the same subproblem reappears. Its whole purpose of existence is 'optimisation'. Here's a very basic example to understand dynamic programming: Fibonacci series.

In the Fibonacci sequence, each number is the sum of the two preceding ones, usually starting with 0 and 1. That is, 'F(0) =

0', 'F(1) = 1' and 'F(n) = F(n-1) + F(n-2)' for n > 1. It implies that to get the value of 'F(n)', we first find the values of 'F(n-1)' and 'F(n-2)' and then add them to get 'F(n)'. This problem can be solved with dynamic programming using a process called tabulation (bottom-up approach), where you solve all related subproblems first in order.

Let's write it in Python:

```python
# Dynamic programming implementation of Fibonacci sequence in Python
    using tabulation

def fibonacci(n):
    # Create a table to store results of subproblems
    fib_table = [0, 1] + [0] * (n - 1)

    # Bottom Up filling of the Fibonacci numbers
    for i in range(2, n+1):
        fib_table[i] = fib_table[i-1] + fib_table[i-2]

    return fib_table[n]

# Test the function
print(fibonacci(7)) # It should print 13
print(fibonacci(9)) # It should print 34
```

Here, we create a table 'fib_table[n+1]' and fill the table using the iterative bottom-up approach. We fill 'fib_table[0]' and 'fib_table[1]' as the basic cases, then we calculate and fill up the table from 'fib_table[2]' to 'fib_table[n]' using the formula 'F(n) = F(n-1) + F(n-2)'. Finally, 'fib_table[n]' has the Fibonacci number for 'n'.

This approach has a time complexity of $O(n)$ which is an improvement from the traditional recursive approach that has a time complexity of $O(2^n)$. The table-building (tabulation) dynamic programming approach allows overlapping subproblems to be computed and stored once, and then having the results readily available to be used in subsequent computations.

4.2   Minimum Coin Change Problem (Bottom-Up Approach)

Minimum Coin Change is a typical example of a problem that can be solved efficiently using Dynamic Programming. Considering that we have a set of denominations and a target amount, the task is to find the minimum number of coins you need to form that target amount. If no combination can sum to the target amount, return -1 (or a specified value). For example, if the target amount is 11 and the denominations are [1, 2, 5], the minimum number of coins required would be 3 (5 + 5 + 1 or 5 + 2 + 2 + 2).

This problem appears simple, but the optimal solution is far from straightforward. Therefore, it requires to be broken down into subproblems, which is a main feature of dynamic programming approach.

The Python solution using the bottom-up approach would be:

```
def coinChange(coins, amount):
    # We use this array to save the answer to subproblems.
    dp = [float('inf')] * (amount + 1)
    # 0 amount can be made by 0 coins.
    dp[0] = 0
    # iterate through all the coins.
    for coin in coins:
        # start from the value of the coin because any amount less
            than this coin can not be made by this coin.
        for x in range(coin, amount + 1):
            # find minimum by not using the coin or using it.
            dp[x] = min(dp[x], dp[x - coin] + 1)
    # If dp[amount] is inf it means we do not have answer so return
        -1 else dp[amount] will have our answer.
    return dp[amount] if dp[amount] != float('inf') else -1
```

The above function starts by initialising a dynamic programming (dp) array of size amount + 1, filled with 'inf', which represents the worst case scenario, where the amount is not reachable from the given coins. 0 coins are needed for '0' amount. For each coin, it checks all the amounts greater than or equal to the coin value, and updates the minimum number of coins needed to reach this amount by not using the current coin, or by using it. The latter case means considering the optimal solution for reaching the amount of 'x - coin' and just adding '1' (the current coin). Finally, it checks whether the amount is reachable or not. If it's not, it return -1.

Since every subproblem is solved exactly once and it requires O(amount) to calculate one state, the total time complexity is O(number of denominations * amount).

4.3 Climbing Stairs Problem with Tabulation

Let's consider a problem where you are climbing a staircase. You begin with being on the ground level (0th stair). From a given stair, you are allowed to climb either one step or two steps up the staircase and there are N stairs in total. The problem is to find the total number of distinct ways to reach the Nth stair.

Here is a simple Python solution using a bottom-up tabulation method to solve this problem:

```
def climbStairs(n):
    '''
    Function to calculate the number of ways to climb a staircase
        with n stairs
    This function uses bottom-up tabulation method of dynamic
        programming
    Time complexity of this function is O(n) and it uses O(n) extra
        space
    '''
```

```
# Tabulation table to store the number of ways for all stairs up
    to n
table = [0]*(n+1)

# Base cases: there is 1 way to climb stair 0 (do nothing) and
    stair 1
table[0] = 1
table[1] = 1

# Calculate the number of ways for all stairs from 2 through n
# For each stair i, the number of ways to climb it is the sum of
# the number of ways to climb stair i-1 (by taking one step)
# and the number of ways to climb stair i-2 (by taking two steps
    )
for i in range(2, n+1):
    table[i] = table[i-1] + table[i-2]

return table[n] # Return the number of ways to climb the nth
    stair
```

This function first initializes a table (a list) of size n+1 with all
0s. The table[i] denotes the number of ways to climb the ith
stair, and table[n] will be our answer. We can easily solve the
base cases, i.e., table[0] = table[1] = 1, because there is only one
way to climb stair 0 (do nothing) and stair 1. After that, we
iteratively calculate table[i] for all 2   i   n using the recurrence
relation:

```
table[i] = table[i - 1] + table[i - 2]
```

We take one step from the (i-1)th stair or two steps from the
(i-2)th stair to reach the ith stair, hence the number of ways to
climb stair i is simply the sum of the number of ways to climb
stair i-1 and stair i-2. In the end, we return table[n] as our final
result.

Note, this dynamic programming approach is much more efficient than the naive recursive approach that has exponential
time complexity due to repeated calculations.

Chapter 5

Solving Classical Dynamic Programming Problems

5.1 Knapsack Problem

The example problem we're dealing with today is a commonly used example in dynamic programming, known as the Knapsack Problem. Here is a brief description of the problem - Suppose you are a thief, robbing a store. The store has different items, each with a certain weight and value. You have a knapsack that can only hold a certain weight. The question is, what items should you steal in order to maximize total value, while keeping the total weight of stolen items less than the capacity of your knapsack? In this problem, we are asked to determine the maximum possible value we can steal, given an array of weights and an array of values (corresponding to each item), and an integer (representing the maximum weight the knapsack can carry).

Here is the Python solution:

```python
def knapSack(W, wt, val, n):
    # Creating a 2D array to store the maximum value
    # obtained for each n and W.
    K = [[0 for w in range(W + 1)]
            for i in range(n + 1)]

    # Build table K[][] in bottom
    # up manner
    for i in range(n + 1):
        for w in range(W + 1):
            # base case
            if i == 0 or w == 0:
                K[i][w] = 0

            # If weight of the nth item is
            # more than Knapsack of capacity W,
            # then this item cannot be included
            # in the optimal solution
            elif wt[i - 1] <= w:
                # Obtain the maximum of two cases:
                # (1) nth item included
                # (2) not included
                K[i][w] = max(val[i - 1]
                    + K[i - 1][w - wt[i - 1]],
                              K[i - 1][w])
            else:
                # If weight of the nth item is more than
                # Knapsack's weight, then move onto
                # the next item
                K[i][w] = K[i - 1][w]

    # K[n][W] is going to hold the maximum
    # value that can be carried in the knapsack
    return K[n][W]

# Driver code
val = [60, 100, 120]
wt = [10, 20, 30]
W = 50
n = len(val)

print(knapSack(W, wt, val, n))
```

The knapSack function above calculates the maximum achievable value by stealing items. The function takes in four parameters: 'W' - knapsack capacity, 'wt' - list representing the weights of the items, 'val' - values of the items, and 'n' - number of items.

We solve this problem by 'remembering' solutions to sub-problems using a table 'K[][]'. 'K[i][w]' represents the maximum value that can be stolen with an available weight capacity of 'w' and the first 'i' items. If the weight of the 'i'th item exceeds 'w', this item cannot be part of the solution and we then consider the previous item. If addition of the 'i'th item doesn't exceed the total weight, then we select the maximum value by either selecting the value of the previous item or the value of the 'i'th item plus the maximum value obtained from the remaining capacity after including the 'i'th item.

The execution time of this solution is 'O(nW)', where 'n' is the number of items and 'W' is the capacity of knapsack.

5.2   Longest Common Subsequence Problem

The Longest Common Subsequence (LCS) problem is a classic computer science problem that deals with finding the longest subsequence that two sequences have in common. The sequences do not need to occupy consecutive positions within the original sequences, hence it is a 'subsequence', not 'substring'. Dynamic programming is a very suitable approach to solve the LCS problem due to its overlapping subproblem structure. The main idea is based on the observation that the LCS of two sequences essentially depends on the LCS of their prefixes. Mathematically, if $X = x1, x2, ..., xm$ and $Y = y1, y2, ..., yn$ are two sequences, and $Z = z1, z2, ..., zk$ is their LCS, then if $xm = yn$, $zk = xm = yn$ and $Zk-1$ is an LCS of $Xm-1$ and $Yn-1$; if $xm != yn$, Zk is LCS of either Xm and $Yn-1$ or $Xm-1$ and Yn.

Python solution for the LCS problem using dynamic programming:

```python
def lcs(X, Y):
    # find the length of the strings
    m = len(X)
    n = len(Y)

    # declaring the array for storing the dp values
    L = [[0]*(n+1) for i in range(m+1)]

    for i in range(m+1):
        for j in range(n+1):
            if i == 0 or j == 0 :
                L[i][j] = 0
            elif X[i-1] == Y[j-1]:
                L[i][j] = L[i-1][j-1]+1
            else:
                L[i][j] = max(L[i-1][j], L[i][j-1])

    # L[m][n] contains the length of LCS of X[0..n-1] & Y[0..m-1]
    return L[m][n]
# end of function lcs

X = "ABCDE"
Y = "ACDFE"
print("Length of LCS is ", lcs(X, Y))
```

In the code, the function lcs(X, Y) solves the problem. It starts by determining the lengths of the input sequences X and Y. It then initializes a 2D array L, with dimensions $(m+1) * (n+1)$, to store the lengths of the longest common subsequences of prefixes of X and Y. The double loops iterate over the elements of L in a bottom-up manner, filling each element based on the given recurrence relation. When it meets X[i] equals to Y[j], it extends the length of LCS from i-1 and j-1. When it meets X[i]

doesn't equal to Y[j], it takes the max LCS length from i-1 and
j or i and j-1. Factors that control the computation are the last
characters of X and Y and whether they match or not. Finally,
L[m][n] gives the length of the LCS of the complete sequences
X and Y.

5.3   Matrix Chain Multiplication Problem

**Matrix Chain Multiplication (MCM) is a problem that
we define in a dynamic programming scenario. Given
a sequence of matrices, the goal of the MCM problem
is to find the most efficient way to multiply these matrices. Since matrix multiplication is associative, the
order in which we multiply matrices does not change
the result, but it can impact the computational cost significantly. The goal is to find the parenthesization of
a product of matrices that minimizes the total number
of scalar multiplications.**

In the solution of the MCM problem, we use dynamic programming. The idea is to keep solving the smaller sub-problems
and use their results to solve bigger problems. The problem
is not straightforward due to the fact that the problem isn't a
simple top-down or bottom-up dynamic programming problem,
but rather it can be broken down into smaller sub-problems in
a somewhat "diagonal" manner.

```
import sys

# Matrix Ai has dimension arr[i-1] x arr[i]
# for i = 1..n

# Function for Matrix Chain Multiplication
def MatrixChainOrder(arr, i, j):

    if i == j:
```

```
            return 0

        _min = sys.maxsize

        # Recursively compute counts of
        # scalar multiplications when
        # different partitions are chosen and
        # return the minimum count
        for k in range(i, j):

            count = (MatrixChainOrder(arr, i, k)
                + MatrixChainOrder(arr, k+1, j)
                    + arr[i-1]*arr[k]*arr[j])

            if (count < _min):
                _min = count;

        # Return minimum count
        return _min;
    # DP approach for MCM problem
    def matrix_chain_order(arr):
        n = len(arr)

        # Creating a matrix to store the intermediate results
        dp = [[0 for _ in range(n)] for _ in range(n)]

        # Filling the dp matrix in a bottom-up.

        for L in range(2, n):
            for i in range(1, n - L + 1):
                j = i + L - 1;
                dp[i][j] = sys.maxsize
                for k in range(i, j):
                    dp[i][j] = min(dp[i][j], dp[i][k] + dp[k + 1][j] + arr
                        [i - 1] * arr[k] * arr[j])

        return dp[1][n - 1]
    # Driver code
    arr = [1, 2, 3, 4, 3]
    n = len(arr)

    print("Minimum number of multiplications is ",
                    matrix_chain_order(arr))
```

In this code, we first define a function MatrixChainOrder(arr, i, j) that takes a list of matrices dimensions, and two indices i and j which represent the range of matrices to consider in the list. We call this function recursively to check each possible partition of the matrices and choose the one that requires the least number of multiplications, which we store in _min. The count of multiplications for each partition is calculated by the formula arr[i-1]*arr[k]*arr[j] + MatrixChainOrder(arr, i, k) + MatrixChainOrder(arr, k+1, j).

The dynamic programming approach avoids recomputation of overlapping subproblems by storing the results of previously solved subproblems in a 2D array dp. The function matrix_chain_order(arr) initializes a nxn matrix dp where n is the number of matrices (or the size of arr), then uses a bottom-up approach to fill in the number of minimum multiplications needed to multiply the chain of matrices from i to j for all possible values of i and j, using the formula dp[i][k] + dp[k + 1][j] + arr[i - 1] * arr[k] * arr[j]. Finally, dp[1][n - 1] gives the minimum number of multiplications needed to multiply the entire sequence of matrices.

Chapter 6

Advanced Dynamic Programming Problems

6.1 Travelling Salesman Problem

Traveling Salesman Problem (TSP) is the classic algorithmic problem focusing on optimization. In the problem, a salesman is given a list of cities, and must determine the shortest route that allows him to visit every city exactly once and return to his original location. The TSP belongs to the class of NP-hard problems in combinatorial optimization, important in operations research and theoretical computer science. We are tasked to minimize the total travel distance.

This problem can be solved using Dynamic Programming (DP). DP is a method for solving a complex problem by breaking it down into simpler subproblems, solving the subproblems just once, and storing their solutions using a memory-based data structure (array, table, etc.). If the same subproblem is encountered again, instead of re-computing its solution, one simply looks up the previously computed solution, thereby saving computation time.

Let's consider the following cities:

```
|     | A  | B  | C  | D  |
|-----|----|----|----|----|
| **A** | 0  | 10 | 15 | 20 |
| **B** | 10 | 0  | 35 | 25 |
| **C** | 15 | 35 | 0  | 30 |
| **D** | 20 | 25 | 30 | 0  |
```

This can be solved using the following Python code:

```python
import numpy as np

# Cities distance
distance = [[0, 10, 15, 20], [10, 0, 35, 25], [15, 35, 0, 30], [20,
    25, 30, 0]]
n = 4

# np.masked_greater creates a masked array and masks all data
    greater than given value
dp = np.full((2**n, n), np.inf)
path = np.full((2**n, n, n), -1)

# Marks first city as visited by setting 1 at 0-th index
visited = 1

# We start at first city, hence distance is zero
dp[visited][0] = 0

# This loop will fix the ending city
for _ in range(n - 1):
    temp_dp = np.full((2**n,n),np.inf)
    temp_path = np.full((2**n, n, n), -1)

    # For every submask in mask
    for mask in range(2**n):
        for node in range(n):
            if mask&(1<<node):
                # If this node was visited
                for i in range(n):
                    # For every node
```

```
                        if mask&(1<<i) and dp[mask][node] + distance[
                            node][i] < temp_dp[mask|(1<<i)][i]:
                            # If `i` is in this mask and taking this
                              step is minimum
                            temp_dp[mask|(1<<i)][i] = dp[mask][node] +
                              distance[node][i]
                            temp_path[mask|(1<<i)][i] = node

            dp = np.copy(temp_dp)
            path = np.copy(temp_path)
    mask = 2**n - 1
    journey = []
    i = np.argmin(dp[-1])

    while(i!=-1):
        journey.append(i)
        mask = mask^(1<<i)
        i = path[mask][i]

    # printing path
    print(journey[::-1])
```

Here, we start at city 0 (A) and calculate the total distance to
all other cities. We track the ending city and the total mask
of visited cities in a dynamic programming (dp) matrix. For
each possible ending city, we iterate through every other city
and if this city is visited, we calculate the total distance. If
it's less than the stored value, we update it. We then set the
ending city as visited and repeat the process. For getting the
path, we backtrack from the city with the shortest distance.
The solution provides the shortest path to visit all cities.

Keep in mind, this problem grows exponentially with the number of cities ($O(n^2 * 2^n)$ for time complexity and $O(n * 2^n)$ for
space complexity), so it's not suitable for large inputs.

6.2 Egg Dropping Puzzle

The Egg Dropping Puzzle is a well-known example of dynamic programming. In this problem, you are given two identical eggs and access to a building with N floors. The task is to find out the highest floor from which the egg can be dropped without breaking it. The puzzle is about determining the minimum maximum number of attempts you need to figure this out. In the worst-case scenario, you would have to drop the egg from every floor starting from the 1st and up to N, so in the worst case, the number of attempts is N. However, we want to find the strategy that minimizes this worst case scenario, which is where dynamic programming comes in.

In Python, a dynamic programming solution for this problem could be written as follows:

```python
def eggDrop(n, k):
    # If there are no floors, then no trials needed.
    # Otherwise, if there is one floor, one trial needed.
    if k == 1 or k == 0:
        return k

    # If there is only one egg available, then the worst case
        scenario is
    # dropping it from each floor one by one, for a total of n
        trials
    if n == 1:
        return k

    min_val = float('inf') # Initializing the minimum value with
        infinity

    # Consider all droppings from 1st to kth floor and
    # recur for the remaining floors. We take the maximum value
        because we're
    # interested in the worst case scenario
    for x in range(1, k+1):
        res = max(eggDrop(n-1, x-1), eggDrop(n, k-x)) # res captures
            the maximum number of trials
        if res < min_val: # Keep track of the minimum number of
            trials
            min_val = res
```

```
    return min_val + 1 # +1 because including this attempt
# Driver program to test the above function
n = 2
k = 10
print("Minimum number of trials in worst case with %d eggs and %d
    floors is %d" % (n, k, eggDrop(n, k)))
```

Note that this implementation has an exponential time complexity because we're making multiple recursive calls to the 'eggDrop' function with the same parameters multiple times (which results in redundant calculations). We could optimize it by storing the results of the subproblems in a lookup table (this is the essence of dynamic programming), so we can simply return the stored result when a function is called again with the same parameters.

In addition to the Python code, to demonstrate the difference between sequential and optimal approaches, you could illustrate the problem with a graph. Here's a simple ASCII-art diagram, where 'x' represents a dropped egg and '|' represents an intact egg:

Sequential (worst case: 10 attempts):

```
10 |
9  |
8  |
7  |
6  |
5  x
4  |
3  |
2  |
1  |
```

Optimal (worst case: 4 attempts):

```
10 |
9  x
8  |
7  |
6  |
5  x
4  |
3  |
2  x
1  |
```

6.3   Optimal Strategy for a Game

Consider a row of n coins of values v1, v2, ..., vn, where n is even. We play a game against an opponent by alternating turns. In each turn, a player selects either the first or last coin from the row, removes it from the row permanently, and receives the value of the coin. Determine the maximum possible amount of money we can definitely win if we move first.

In Python, we will solve the problem using dynamic programming, specifically a 2D DP approach. We create a 2D table where each cell DP[i][j] represents the optimal amount of money that a player can collect from i'th coin to j'th coin. The DP solution will fill this table in a bottom-up manner.

```python
# Optimal Strategy for a Game

def optimalStrategyOfGame(arr, n):
    # Create a table to store solutions of subproblems
    dp = [[0 for i in range(n)] for i in range(n)]

    # Fill table using recursive formula
    # Note that the table is filled in diagonal fashion, from
    #     diagonal elements to table[0][n-1]
    for gap in range(n):
        for j in range(gap, n):
            i = j - gap
```

```
# Here x is value of F(i+2, j), y is F(i+1, j-1) and z is
    F(i, j-2) in above recursive formula
x = 0
if((i + 2) <= j):
    x = dp[i + 2][j]
y = 0
if((i + 1) <= (j - 1)):
    y = dp[i + 1][j - 1]
z = 0
if(i <= (j - 2)):
    z = dp[i][j - 2]
dp[i][j] = max(arr[i] + min(x, y), arr[j] + min(y, z))

    # The optimal amount a player can win is stored at dp[0][n-1]
    return dp[0][n - 1]
# Test the optimalStrategyOfGame function
arr1 = [8, 15, 3, 7]
n = len(arr1)
print('nMaximum possible amount player's optimal strategy can win =
    ', optimalStrategyOfGame(arr1, n))
```

In the above Python code, we first create a 2D matrix 'dp'. The value 'dp[i][j]' will be the maximum value that Player 1 can collect from coin i to coin j. The possible moves are to choose the i-th coin or the j-th coin. Player 1 will make the move that maximises his score. Player 2 aims at minimizing Player 1's amount, so he will always choose the lower value. This strategy allows the first player to choose the maximum possible amount.

The dynamic programing concept implemented here is overlapping subproblems, as the same coins might be considered multiple times. The memoization, in the form of a 2D DP matrix, helps in storing previous computed values, improving efficiency significantly.

This method will yield the correct solution because it guarantees the optimal strategy for each player at every stage of the game. The final answer is stored at dp[0][n-1], which is the maximum amount Player 1 can win when all coins from 0 to n-1 are available.

Chapter 7

Dynamic Programming in Graph Problems

7.1 Shortest Path in a Graph using Bellman-Ford Algorithm

The Bellman-Ford Algorithm is an algorithm that computes shortest paths from a single source vertex to all of the other vertices in a weighted digraph, it works even for graphs with negative-weight edges. It's named after its developers, Richard Bellman and Lester Ford. The main idea behind Bellman-Ford is to relax all edges exactly n-1 times, where n is the number of vertices in the graph. 'Relaxation' in this context simply means to update the shortest paths. After doing this relaxation process n-1 times, we get all shortest path to all vertices, however, after the nth time, if we can relax any

edge, it means there is a negative cycle in the graph.

Here is an implementation of the Bellman-Ford algorithm in Python:

```python
def bellman_ford_algorithm(graph, source):
    # Step 1: Prepare the distance for each node
    distance, predecessor = dict(), dict()
    for node in graph:
        distance[node], predecessor[node] = float('inf'), None
    distance[source] = 0

    # Step 2: Relax the edges
    for _ in range(len(graph) - 1):
        for node in graph:
            for neighbour in graph[node]:
                # If the distance between the node and the neighbour
                    is lower than the current, store it
                if distance[node] + graph[node][neighbour] < distance[
                    neighbour]:
                    distance[neighbour], predecessor[neighbour] =
                        distance[node] + graph[node][neighbour], node

    # Step 3: Check for negative weight cycles
    for node in graph:
        for neighbour in graph[node]:
            assert distance[node] + graph[node][neighbour] >= distance
                [neighbour], "Negative weight cycle."

    return distance, predecessor

# representation of the graph in python
graph = {
    'a': {'b': -1, 'c': 4},
    'b': {'c': 3, 'd': 2, 'e': 2},
    'c': {},
    'd': {'b': 1, 'c': 5},
    'e': {'d': -3}
    }

bellman_ford_algorithm(graph, 'a')
```

This program starts by initializing the distance to the source to 0 and all other nodes to infinity. Then it relaxes(allows to make shorter) the distances by travelling edges and updates the minimum distance if a shorter path was found. It does this for all the vertices '|V|-1' times where '|V|' is the number of vertices, as in the worst case, a shortest path may need to traverse all vertices. The last step is to loop over all edges again and if we can still relax the edges that means we have a negative cycle.

7.2   Counting Paths in a Directed Acyclic Graph

The problem we are considering is the number of unique paths that exist in a Directed Acyclic Graph (DAG) from a given node 's' to another node 't'. A DAG is a directed graph with no directed cycles - that is, it's impossible to start at some vertex 'v' and follow a sequence of directed edges that eventually loops back to 'v'. The task is to compute the number of unique paths from 's' to 't'.

First of all, we'll need to represent our graph somehow. The easiest way to do this is with an adjacency list, where each node 'i' has a list of neighbors it's adjacent to. Then we will create two arrays: dist and paths. The dist array will help us to keep track of the shortest path between node 's' and every other node, whereas the paths array will be used to count the number of paths between 's' and every other node.

```
def num_of_paths(graph, s, t):
    # Initializing the dist and paths arrays
    dist = [float('inf')] * len(graph)
    paths = [0] * len(graph)
    dist[s] = 0
    paths[s] = 1

    # Topological sort
    topo_order = topological_sort(graph)

    for u in topo_order:
        # Relaxing all the adjacent vertices of u
        for v in graph[u]:
            if dist[v] > dist[u] + 1: # If we have found a shorter
```

```
                 path, then update the dist[v] and paths[v]
              dist[v] = dist[u] + 1
              paths[v] = paths[u]
           elif dist[v] == dist[u] + 1: # If another shortest path is
              found, then add the paths[u] to paths[v]
              paths[v] += paths[u]

    return paths[t]

def topological_sort(graph):
    # Assuming the graph is a DAG, we just need to return a list of
        vertices sorted by postvisit numbers.
    # This can be done with DFS in a straightforward manner.
    stack = []
    visited = set()
    for v in range(len(graph)):
        if v not in visited:
            dfs(graph, v, visited, stack)
    return stack[::-1] # reversing the list as we want it in
        descending order

def dfs(graph, v, visited, stack):
    visited.add(v)
    for u in graph[v]:
        if u not in visited:
            dfs(graph, u, visited, stack)
    stack.append(v)
```

This algorithm employs the topological sort and uses Dynamic
Programming (DP) to solve the problem. The time complexity
of the algorithm is 'O($N + M$)' where 'N' is the number of
vertices and 'M' is the number of edges in the graph. The
space complexity is 'O(N)'.

7.3   Maximum Flow in a Graph with Ford-Fulkerson Algorithm

The problem can be described as finding the maximum
possible flow in a directed graph where every edge has
a capacity. In this problem, also known as a Maximum
Flow problem, we aim to maximize the flow from a

source node to a sink node under the constraint that
the flow along an edge cannot exceed its given capacity.
Ford Fulkerson method or algorithm, developed by L.R
Ford Jr. and D.R Fulkerson, is a greedy approach for
calculating the maximum flow in a graph. The steps
in this algorithm involve finding a path from source
to sink, sending flow along this path, and then finding
another path. This procedure continues until we can
no longer find a valid path from source to sink.

Python Code:

```python
# Defining the Graph class to initialize an empty graph
class Graph:
    def __init__(self, vertices):
        self.V = vertices
        self.graph = [[0 for _ in range(vertices)] for _ in range(
            vertices)]

# Checking if there is any path from source to sink
def BFS(self, source, sink, parent):
    visited = [False] * self.V
    queue = []
    queue.append(source)
    visited[source] = True

    while queue:
        u = queue.pop(0)
        for ind, val in enumerate(self.graph[u]):
            if visited[ind] == False and val > 0:
                queue.append(ind)
                visited[ind] = True
                parent[ind] = u
                if ind == sink:
                    return True
    return False

# Applying fordFulkerson algorithm
def FordFulkerson(self, source, sink):

    parent = [-1] * self.V
    max_flow = 0

    while self.BFS(source, sink, parent):

        path_flow = float("Inf")
        s = sink

        while(s != source):
```

```
            path_flow = min(path_flow, self.graph[parent[s]][s])
            s = parent[s]

        max_flow += path_flow

        v = sink
        while(v != source):
            u = parent[v]
            self.graph[u][v] -= path_flow
            self.graph[v][u] += path_flow
            v = parent[v]

    return max_flow
```

This Python code first creates a graph. The class 'Graph' contains the edge weights (graph), the number of vertices (V), and two methods: 'BFS' and 'FordFulkerson'. The 'BFS' function checks if there is a path from the source to the sink. The 'Ford-Fulkerson' function calculates the maximum flow in the graph. In each iteration of the while loop, the function checks for a path from the source to the sink, computes the path with minimum residual capacity ('path_flow'), adds this minimum capacity to the total maximum flow ('max_flow'), and then updates the residual capacities of the edges. This iteration continues until no augmenting path is found in the residual graph. Finally, it returns the 'max_flow' which is the maximum flow in the graph.

Chapter 8

Space Optimization in Dynamic Programming

8.1 Space-Efficient Fibonacci Series

The problem we're dealing with here is known as the "Fibonacci Sequence". Starting from 0 and 1, each number in this sequence is the sum of the two numbers immediately preceding it. For example, the start of the sequence is 0, 1, 1, 2, 3, 5, 8, 13, 21, and so forth. We're posed with the question of how to use Dynamic Programming in Python to compute the Fibonacci sequence in a way that is efficient in terms of memory usage. Instead of storing all previously computed values of the sequence, we wish to only store the last two values. The mathematical formula for the Fibonacci sequence can be written as $F(n) = F(n-1) +$

F(n-2), where F(n) is the nth number in the Fibonacci sequence.

Here is a Python code example for a space-efficient implementation of Fibonacci sequence using dynamic programming:

```
def fibonacci(n):
    # cases for n equals to 0 or 1
    if n == 0:
        return 0
    elif n == 1:
        return 1
    a, b = 0, 1
    for _ in range(2, n+1):
        # dynamic programming, saving just the last two numbers
        a, b = b, a + b
    return b

print(fibonacci(10))
```

In this code, we initialize two variables, 'a' and 'b', to represent F(n-2) and F(n-1), respectively. Then, for each number from 2 to 'n', we compute the next number in the sequence, update 'a' and 'b' for the next iteration. This approach saves significantly on memory as it only requires storing the two most recent numbers in the sequence. The result of 'fibonacci(10)' is '55', which is the 10th number in the Fibonacci sequence.

Note: The initial condition of this function handles the cases where 'n' is 0 or 1, because the Fibonacci sequence is only defined for 'n' >= 2.

8.2   Optimizing Space in 0/1 Knapsack Problem

The 0-1 Knapsack problem is a classic optimization problem in computer science where the goal is to max-

imize the total value of a set of items, given that the
total weight of the items should not exceed a certain
limit. Each item is characterized by its weight and
value. The problem is called 0-1 Knapsack because
each item can either be taken completely or not taken
at all, there can't be fractions.

Dynamic programming is usually employed to solve this problem since it has overlapping subproblems and optimal substructure.

```
def knapSack(W, wt, val, n):
    """
    Function to solve 0-1 Knapsack problem using Dynamic Programming
        Approach
    Args:
        W: total weight that the knapsack can hold
        wt: list of weights of each item
        val: list of values of each item
        n: total number of items
    Returns:
        max value that can be put in knapsack of capacity W
    """
    K = [[0 for w in range(W + 1)]
        for i in range(n + 1)]

    # Building K[n][w] in bottom up manner
    for i in range(n + 1):
        for w in range(W + 1):
            if i == 0 or w == 0:
                K[i][w] = 0
            elif wt[i - 1] <= w:
                # Find the maximum of not picking the i-th item and
                    picking the i-th item
                K[i][w] = max(val[i - 1]
                    + K[i - 1][w - wt[i - 1]],
                            K[i - 1][w])
            else:
                K[i][w] = K[i - 1][w]

    return K[n][W]

# test the function
val = [60, 100, 120]
wt = [10, 20, 30]
W = 50
n = len(val)

print(knapSack(W, wt, val, n))
```

The function 'knapSack' initializes a 2-D list 'K' which has '(n+1)' rows and '(W+1)' columns. 'K[i][w]' represents the maximum value that can be achieved with weight 'w' using items up to 'i'. For each item, we either include the item in the optimal subset or discard it. If the item's weight does not exceed 'w', we find the maximum of the value we get from including the item and the value from not including it, otherwise we can't include the item. Finally, 'K[n][W]' will hold the maximum value that can be achieved with a weight of 'W'.

8.3 Space-optimized Longest Common Subsequence Problem

The Longest Common Subsequence (LCS) problem is a classic computer science problem that asks "given two sequences, X and Y, find the maximum-length common subsequence of X and Y." A subsequence is a sequence that appears in the same order, but not necessarily consecutively, in another sequence. For example, given two sequences like "ABCBDAB" and "BDCAB", the longest common subsequence is "BCAB". Solving it dynamically, instead of using brute force, will save computational resources. However, the traditional dynamic programming solution uses a 2D array of size m x n (where m and n are the lengths of the two input strings) which can be space-expensive. We can optimize this using dynamic programming and only two rows (current and previous) instead of a full m x n matrix.

The Python solution is as follows:

```python
def lcs(X , Y):
    # Find lengths of two strings
    m = len(X)
    n = len(Y)

    # Create a 2D list to store results of subproblems
    dp = [[0 for j in range(n+1)] for i in range(2)]

    # Fill dp[][] in bottom-up manner
    # i%2 will be always 1 and (i-1)%2 will be always 0 (for i > 0)
    for i in range(m+1):
        for j in range(n+1):
            if i == 0 or j == 0:
                dp[i%2][j] = 0
            elif X[i-1] == Y[j-1]:
                dp[i%2][j] = dp[(i-1)%2][j-1] + 1
            else:
                dp[i%2][j] = max(dp[(i-1)%2][j], dp[i%2][j-1])

    # Length of LCS is dp[m%2][n]
    return dp[m%2][n]

# Test the function
X = "ABCBDAB"
Y = "BDCAB"
print("Length of LCS is ", lcs(X, Y))
```

This Python script works by creating a 2D list (dp[][]) and iteratively filling it in a bottom-up manner. The 2D list stores the results of subproblems, which are essentially the lengths of longest common subsequences for different substrings of X and Y. Here, i and j denote the indices of X and Y respectively. If the characters at index i in X and index j in Y are the same (X[i-1] == Y[j-1]), the length of the LCS till i and j would be the length of the LCS till i-1 and j-1, plus 1 (dp[i%2][j] = dp[(i-1)%2][j-1] + 1). If not, the length of the LCS would be the maximum of LCS till i-1 and LCS till i (dp[i%2][j] = max(dp[(i-1)%2][j], dp[i%2][j-1])). This way, we keep filling the 2D list iteratively, hence solving the subproblems and eventually the main problem (the length of LCS for complete sequences X and Y) by the end of the process. The use of i%2 and (i-1)%2 helps to limit the space complexity to just two rows, which makes it space-optimized.

Chapter 9

State and Transition in Dynamic Programming

9.1 Building an Intuition for States with Grid-Traveler Problem

The grid traveler problem is a classical computer science problem that falls within a class of problems susceptible to solution by dynamic programming. For instance, consider a 2-dimensional grid, where the size of the grid is m*n, m and n are positive integers. A traveler is sitting at the top-left corner of the grid and their aim is to reach the bottom-right corner. However, they can only move down or right. The question then is: In how many ways can the traveler reach the destination?

To solve this problem using Dynamic programming in Python, you would set up and solve a system of recurrence relations. You would begin by initializing an m by n array with all elements as zero which describes the number of ways to get to each point in the grid. The following code shows this in Python:

```python
def gridTraveler(m, n):
    # Initialized m*n array/table with all elements as zero
    memo = [[0 for _ in range(n+1)] for _ in range(m+1)]
    memo[1][1] = 1 # base case (when m and n are 1)

    # Loop through the 2-D memo array
    for i in range(m+1):
        for j in range(n+1):
            # Updating the number of ways of the down cell (if it
                exists)
            if i+1 <= m:
                memo[i+1][j] += memo[i][j]
            # Updating the number of ways of the right cell (if it
                exists)
            if j+1 <= n:
                memo[i][j+1] += memo[i][j]

    return memo[m][n]

m = 3
n = 3
print(gridTraveler(m, n)) # Output: 6
```

In this solution, we start at the top left of the grid, which has been pre-populated with a ''1'' since there is only 1 way to get to the starting point. The gridTraveler function loops through each cell in the grid. For each current cell, the function checks if there is a cell below it (if 'i+1' is less than or equal to 'm') and if there is, it adds the number of ways of reaching the current cell to the cell below it. The function does the same for the cell to the right (if 'j+1' is less than or equal to 'n') of the current cell. The returned value (after traversing the grid) of the function is the number of ways to travel from the top left to the bottom right of the grid.

Remember, there is no "one right way" to solve dynamic programming problems. This method is just one of many, but it's a good start for learning dynamic programming.

9.2 Understanding Transitions with Subset Sum Problem

The subset sum problem is a decision problem commonly used in computer science and mathematics. Given a set of non-negative integers, and a target value, the target value must be satisfied by summing values from elements within the provided set. Precisely, given a set, S, of n integers and another integer, x, the subset sum problem is to decide whether there exists a subset of S that adds up exactly to x or not.

Now let's provide a Python solution using dynamic programming. The idea is to construct a table, subset[i][j], that fills 'true' or 'false' values to indicate if there is a subset of set S[0..j-1] with sum equal to i. Our final solution will be subset[sum][n].

```
def isSubsetSum(set, n, sum):
    """
    creates a 2D table using dynamic programming principles
    """
    # table to store subset solutions
    subset = ([[False for i in range(sum + 1)] for i in range(n + 1)
        ])

    # fill 0th row as True
    for i in range(0, n + 1):
        subset[i][0] = True

    # fill 0th column, except first cell, as 0
    for i in range(1, sum + 1):
        subset[0][i]= False

    # fill the table in bottom-up manner
    for i in range(1, n + 1):
```

```
        for j in range(1, sum + 1):
            if j < set[i-1]:
                subset[i][j] = subset[i-1][j]
            if j >= set[i-1]:
                subset[i][j] = (subset[i-1][j] or
                              subset[i - 1][j-set[i-1]])

    # return last value
    return subset[n][sum]

# test function
set = [3, 34, 4, 12, 5, 2]
sum = 9
n = len(set)
if (isSubsetSum(set, n, sum) == True):
    print("Found a subset with given sum")
else:
    print("No subset with given sum")
```

This solution has time complexity of $O(sum * n)$, where sum is the target sum and n is the size of the set. As the sum can be very large and even exceed n in worst case, this becomes inefficient.

9.3   Formulating State and Transition Relations with Job Sequencing Problem

The Job Sequencing problem is a classical problem, where we are given a set of jobs each with a certain deadline and profit to be gained on completion. The task is to schedule these jobs on a single machine in such a way so as to maximize the total profit. The machine can only work on a single job at a time and a job once started must run to completion. Furthermore, a job can only be scheduled before its respective deadline.

For this problem, we can define our state as dp[time], where dp[time] represents the maximum total profit we can achieve by scheduling jobs up until this given point in time. We start with a time of 0 and continue up to the maximum deadline time in the dataset. The transition from one state dp[time] to the next state dp[time+1] will be dependent upon whether it is profitable to schedule a new job at the current time or if it is better to simply continue with the jobs already scheduled.

Here is Python code for implementing a solution to this problem using dynamic programming:

```
from collections import namedtuple
from operator import attrgetter

# Define the Job data structure with deadline and profit
Job = namedtuple('Job', ['deadline', 'profit'])

def schedule(jobs):
    # Sort the jobs by profit in non-increasing order
    jobs.sort(key=attrgetter('profit'), reverse=True)

    # Initialize dp array, dp[i] represents max profit achievable by
        time i
    dp = [0] * (max([job.deadline for job in jobs]) + 1)

    # Iterate over jobs for scheduling
    for job in jobs:
        for time in range(job.deadline, 0, -1):
            # If job can be scheduled at this time without overlapping
                an already scheduled job
            # and it leads to a higher profit, we choose to schedule
                it.
            if dp[time] == 0 or dp[time-1] + job.profit > dp[time]:
                dp[time] = max(dp[time-1] + job.profit, dp[time])
            else:
                # Otherwise, we move to the next time slot
                break

    return dp[-1]

# Testing the code
jobs = [Job(2, 100), Job(1, 19), Job(2, 27), Job(1, 25), Job(3, 15)]
print(schedule(jobs))
```

This prints '142' which is the maximum profit achievable by following an optimal job scheduling.

$$dp[\text{time}] = \begin{cases} \max(dp[\text{time} - 1] + \text{job.profit}, dp[\text{time}]), \\ \quad \text{if } dp[\text{time}] = 0 \text{ or } dp[\text{time} - 1] + \text{job.profit} > dp[\text{time}] \\ dp[\text{time}], \text{ otherwise} \end{cases}$$

To reason about complexity, let's denote 'n' as the number of jobs and 'T' as the maximum deadline. The sorting operation takes 'O($nlogn$)' time. After that, for each task we could potentially scan from 'T' to '1', so in the worst case, the time complexity is 'O(nT)'. Therefore, the overall time complexity is 'O($nlogn + nT$)'. However, in practice, this worst case scenario does not frequently occur because of the breaks in the loop when a job cannot be scheduled.

The space complexity is 'O(T)', as we need an array of size 'T' to track the maximum profit at each point in time.

Chapter 10

Dynamic Programming in String Algorithms

10.1 Edit Distance Problem

The Edit Distance Problem is a classic example in dynamic programming that deals with the problem of transformation from one string to another. The goal is to determine the minimum number of operations (insertions, deletions, and substitutions) required to transform one string into another. Each action carries a cost, which is usually considered equal for simplicity. For instance, transforming the string "kitten" into "sitting" requires 3 operations: substituting 'k' for 's', substituting 'e' for 'i', and appending 'g' at the end. Thus, the edit distance between "kitten" and "sitting" is 3. The problem becomes nontrivial when the strings

are large or when they have many common substrings.

The dynamic programming approach uses a computational solution to iterate over all possibilities and build up the optimal solution.

Here is a Python solution of the Edit Distance Problem using dynamic programming:

```python
def edit_distance(str1, str2):
    """Calculates the minimum number of edits (operations) required
        to convert `str1` into `str2`"""
    len_str1 = len(str1)
    len_str2 = len(str2)

    # Create a matrix (2D list) to store the edit distances
    dp = [[0 for _ in range(len_str2 + 1)] for _ in range(len_str1 +
        1)]

    for i in range(len_str1 + 1):
        for j in range(len_str2 + 1):

            # Filling dp[i][j]: the number of operations to convert
                str1[:i] to str2[:j]

            # Scenario 1: If str1 is empty, all characters of str2
                should be inserted
            if i == 0:
                dp[i][j] = j # Minimum operations = j

            # Scenario 2: If str2 is empty, all characters of str1
                should be removed
            elif j == 0:
                dp[i][j] = i # Minimum operations = i

            # Scenario 3: If last characters of both strings are the
                same, ignore last character
            # because the edit distance is going to be the same as the
                previous strings
            elif str1[i-1] == str2[j-1]:
                dp[i][j] = dp[i-1][j-1]

            # Scenario 4: If last characters are not the same,
                consider all possibilities and choose the minimal one
            else:
                dp[i][j] = 1 + min(
                    dp[i][j-1],      # Insertion
                    dp[i-1][j],      # Removal
                    dp[i-1][j-1]     # Replacement
                )

    return dp[len_str1][len_str2]
```

```
# Driver code
str1 = "kitten"
str2 = "sitting"

print(edit_distance(str1, str2))
```

The program builds a 'dp' table in which dp[i][j] represents the minimum number of operations to convert str1[:i] to str2[:j]. With nested loops, it fills in this table according to the four possible scenarios described in the comments. Note that in the case of different last characters (Scenario 4), I use the 'min' function to select the least costly option from the preceding strings: either by inserting, removing, or replacing a character. In the end, I simply return the distance found in dp[len_str1][len_str2], which represents the distance after checking all characters in both strings.

10.2 Longest Palindromic Subsequence

In the Longest Palindromic Subsequence (LPS) problem, we are given a string (sequence of characters) and the goal is to determine the length of the longest subsequence which is also a palindrome. A subsequence is a sequence that can be derived from another sequence by deleting some or no elements, without changing the order of the remaining elements. A palindrome is a word, phrase, number or other sequences of characters that reads the same forward and backwards (ignoring spaces, punctuation, and capitalization). This problem is a classical example of Dynamic Programming.

Now, let's move on to the Python solution of the problem. Here, the idea used for dynamic programming is to construct a table in a bottom-up manner where each cell of the table includes the length of the longest palindrome subsequence. For substrings of length 1, the length of the LPS is 1. For substrings of length 2, the length of the LPS is 2 if the two characters are the same, and 1 otherwise. For longer substrings, if the end characters of the string are the same, the length is the length of the LPS of the inner substring, plus 2. If the end characters are not the same, the length is the maximum of the LPS of the substrings obtained by removing either the first character or the last character.

Here is the Python code that implements the above approach:

```python
def LPS(str):
    n = len(str)

    # Create a table to store results of subproblems
    L = [[0 for x in range(n)] for x in range(n)]

    # Strings of length 1 are palindrome of length 1
    for i in range(n):
        L[i][i] = 1

    # Build the table. Note that the lower diagonal values of table
        are
    # useless and not filled in the process. The values are filled
        in a
    # manner similar to Matrix Chain Multiplication.
    for cl in range(2, n+1):
        for i in range(n - cl + 1):
            j = i + cl - 1
            if (str[i] == str[j] and cl == 2):
                L[i][j] = 2
            elif (str[i] == str[j]):
                L[i][j] = L[i + 1][j - 1] + 2
            else:
                L[i][j] = max(L[i][j - 1], L[i + 1][j]);

    # length of longest palindromic subsequence
    return L[0][n - 1]

# testing example
input = "BBABCBCAB"
print("The length of the longest palindrome subsequence is", LPS(
    input))
```

Please note that the above implementation prints only the length of LPS, not the subsequence itself. The time complexity of the above solution is $O(n^2)$ where n is the length of the input string.

10.3 Regular Expression Matching

This problem requires you to implement a function that checks if a given text string 's' matches a given regular expression 'p', where 'p' can contain special characters such as '.' and '*'. The special character '.' matches any single character, while '*' matches zero or more of the preceding character. Here are some examples:

- 's = "aab"' and 'p = "c*a*b"' return True
- 's = "mississippi"' and 'p = "mis*is*p*"' returns False

Below is the Python code to solve this problem with explanations about the dynamic programming method utilized.

```python
def isMatch(s: str, p: str) -> bool:
    # Create the dp table and initialize it to False,
    # The size of the table will be len(s)+1 x len(p)+1,
    # additional 1 is added to include empty string/regex
        representation
    dp = [[False] * (len(p) + 1) for _ in range(len(s) + 1)]

    # initialize the base case, two empty strings are matched
    dp[-1][-1] = True

    # Update dp table
    for i in range(len(s), -1, -1):
        for j in range(len(p) - 1, -1, -1):
            # check if the current characters are matching
            match = i < len(s) and p[j] in {s[i], '.'}
            if j+1 < len(p) and p[j+1] == '*':
                # Case when we encounter '*', Here we got two
                    possibilities:
                # 1. We consider zero occurrence of preceding
                    character
                # 2. We are considering more than 1 occurrence of
                    preceding character
                dp[i][j] = dp[i][j+2] or match and dp[i+1][j]
            else:
                # For cases when there is direct match or '.'
                dp[i][j] = match and dp[i+1][j+1]
```

```
    return dp[0][0]
# Test case:
print(isMatch('mississippi', 'mis*is*p*')) # Returns: False
```

Here, we use dynamic programming to avoid redundant computation. A 2-D boolean 'dp' table is created to store the match statuses of substrings of 's' and 'p'. 'dp[i][j]' is True if the substring 's[i:]' matches 'p[j:]', otherwise False.

We fill up this table based on simple match status and considering the effects of wildcard characters. For the special character '*', we look at zero occurrence (hence we see after two characters) and more than one occurrence (hence we see after one character). For simple match or '', we move diagonally as it's one-to-one correspondence.

The final answer is stored in the top-left cell, 'dp[0][0]', because it represents the status of the match between the entire string 's' and 'p'.

Dynamic programming helps speed up the process by storing intermediate results so that they can be reused later, therefore it avoids redundant computation and makes the solution much faster, especially for long strings.

Chapter 11

Dynamic Programming in Computational Geometry

11.1 Largest Rectangle in a Histogram

Let's consider a problem where we have a list 'hist' representing the heights of different bars in a histogram. Our task is to find the largest rectangle that can be formed in this histogram. The width of each given bar is 1, and the height is the number in the list. The rectangle can only be made up of contiguous bars, and it should span vertically. This is a standard problem of Dynamic Programming.

To solve this problem, we will use a stack data structure and go through the given list. The logic behind this is that if the current bar's height is higher than the bar's height on the top of the stack, we push it into the stack. If it's lower, we start removing bars from the stack and calculate the area of the rectangle that can be formed using the bar at the top of the stack.

Here is the python code for this problem:

```python
def max_histogram_area(hist):
    # This function calculates the maximum rectangular area under
        given histrogram with n bars.

    # Create an empty stack to hold indices of hist[] list
    # Stack holds indices of hist[] list where 'bar of histogram' is
        greater than the bar at top of stack
    stack = []

    max_area = 0 # Initialize max area as zero

    index = 0
    while index < len(hist):
        if (not stack) or (hist[stack[-1]] <= hist[index]):
            stack.append(index) # Push to stack if histogram is
                increasing, and increment index
            index += 1
        else:
            # If current bar is lower than top of stack, calculate
                area of rectangle
            # with stack top as the smallest bar or the height of
                rectangle
            top_of_stack = stack.pop()

            # Calculate the area with hist[top_of_stack] as height of
                rectangle
            # and stack holds indices of hist[] list where 'bar of
                histogram' is less than the bar at top of stack
            area = (hist[top_of_stack] *
                ((index - stack[-1] - 1)
                if stack else index))

            max_area = max(max_area, area) # Update max_area value

    # Now pop the remaining bars from stack and calculate area with
        every popped bar as height of rectangle
    while stack:
        top_of_stack = stack.pop()
        area = (hist[top_of_stack] *
            ((index - stack[-1] - 1)
            if stack else index))

        max_area = max(max_area, area) # Update max_area value

    # Return maximum area under the given histogram
```

```
return max_area
```

This code allows us to calculate the maximum rectangular area
in a histogram. You can test this function with a histogram list,
for example 'hist = [6, 2, 5, 4, 5, 1, 6]', the largest rectangle in
this histogram has an area of 12. Call the function with the histogram list as argument prints the area of the largest rectangle,
'print(max_histogram_area(hist))' should return '12'.

This solution has a time complexity of 'O(n)' since we process
every bar once, where 'n' is the number of bars in the histogram.
The space complexity of this solution is also 'O(n)' since in the
worst case we may end up storing all bars in the stack.

I is the input list of heights of bars in the histogram, n is the
number of bars in the histogram, S is the stack used to store
indices of bars, and A is the maximum area of rectangle in the
histogram.

If $I = [6, 2, 5, 4, 5, 1, 6]$, then after processing all bars, $A = 12$.

In this case, the largest rectangle has height 4, and width 3 (it
includes bars with heights 4, 5 and 5), and that's why it gives
the area 12.

11.2   Convex Hull Problem

The Convex Hull problem is an important problem in
computational geometry. Given a set of points in the
plane, the Convex Hull is the smallest convex polygon
that contains all the points. More intuitively, if each
point is imagined as a nail sticking out from a board,

the Convex Hull would be the shape of the tightest
rubber band that could be stretched around all the
nails. In computation, finding the Convex Hull of a set
of points is fundamentally a sorting problem, and it's
widely used in fields like computer graphics, pattern
recognition, image processing, statistics, etc. Multiple algorithms exist to solve this problem and one of
the well-known algorithms is the "Graham's Scan Algorithm".

Here is the Python program which implements the Graham
Scan algorithm to solve the Convex Hull problem:

```python
import matplotlib.pyplot as plt
from functools import cmp_to_key
import numpy as np

# A global point needed for sorting points with reference
p0 = (0, 0)


# A utility function to find next to top in a stack
def nextToTop(S):
    return S[-2]

# A utility function to swap two points
def swap(P, i, j):
    temp = P[i]
    P[i] = P[j]
    P[j] = temp

# A utility function to return square of distance
# between p1 and p2
def distSq(p1, p2):
    return ((p1[0] - p2[0])**2 +
            (p1[1] - p2[1])**2)

# To find orientation of ordered triplet (p1, p2, p3).
def orientation(p1, p2, p3):
    val = (p2[1] - p1[1]) * (p3[0] - p2[0]) -
          (p2[0] - p1[0]) * (p3[1] - p2[1])
    if val == 0:
        return 0
    elif val > 0:
        return 1
    else:
        return 2

# We use the orientation() function defined above to sort the points
```

```python
def comparator(p1, p2):
    o = orientation(p0, p1, p2)
    if o == 0:
        if distSq(p0, p2) >= distSq(p0, p1):
            return -1
        else:
            return 1
    else:
        if o == 2:
            return -1
        else:
            return 1

# Prints convex hull of a set of n points.
def convexHull(points, n):
    global p0
    # Find the bottommost point
    ymin = points[0][1]
    minn = 0
    for i in range(1,n):
        y = points[i][1]
        if (y < ymin) or (ymin == y and points[i][0] < points[minn
            ][0]):
            ymin = points[i][1]
            minn = i

    # Swap the found minimum with first point
    swap(points, 0, minn)

    # Sort remaining points to finish prep stage
    p0 = points[0]
    points = sorted(points, key = cmp_to_key(comparator))

    # Keep removing the top while angle of three consecutive points
        of stack is not turning left
    m = 1
    for i in range(1,n):
        while(i < n-1 and orientation(p0, points[i], points[i+1]) ==
            0):
            i +=1

        points[m] = points[i]
        m += 1

    # Create an empty stack and push first three points to it.
    if m < 3:
        return []

    else:
        S = []
        S.append(points[0])
        S.append(points[1])
        S.append(points[2])

        # Process remaining points
        for i in range(3,m):
            while len(S) > 1 and orientation(nextToTop(S), S[-1],
                points[i]) != 2:
```

```
        S.pop()

        S.append(points[i])

    # Now stack has the output points, so return
    return S
# Test function
points = [(0, 3), (2, 2), (1, 1), (2, 1),
        (3, 0), (0, 0), (3, 3)]
n = len(points)
convex_hull = convexHull(points, n)

print("The points in Convex Hull are: n")
for point in convex_hull:
    print(point)

plt.figure()
plt.scatter(*zip(*points))
plt.scatter(*zip(*convex_hull))
for i in range(len(convex_hull)-1):
    plt.plot(*zip(*[convex_hull[i], convex_hull[i+1]]), 'r-')
plt.plot(*zip(*[convex_hull[len(convex_hull)-1], convex_hull[0]]), '
    r-')
plt.show()
```

This Python program will print the points of Convex Hull in
the set of input points and plot these points using matplotlib
library showing the Convex Hull. More commonly, the Convex
Hull problem is solved as a preprocessing step in many higher-
dimensional algorithms, for example, in the computation of 2D
Voronoi Diagrams.

11.3   Closest Pair of Points Problem

The closest pair of points problem or the closest pair
problem is a well-known problem in Computational Geometry: given a list of n points in a plane, find the
pair of points that has the least Euclidean distance to
each other. This problem can be solved efficiently using
Dynamic Programming. The naive or brute force so-

lution would involve computing the distance between
every pair of points and then choosing the smallest,
which takes $O(n^2)$ time. However, with a Divide and
Conquer approach, the problem can be solved in much
faster manner, i.e., in $O(n(log n)^2)$ time.

Let us now illustrate a code solution using Python. Here is a
step by step solution.

```python
from math import dist
def closest_pair(points, num_of_points):
    '''Find the closest pair of points among the given points'''

    # sort the points according to x coordinates
    points.sort(key = lambda K: K[0])

    #Use the recursive function to find the smallest distance
    return closest_pair_recursive(points, num_of_points)

def closest_pair_recursive(points, num_of_points):
    '''A recursive function to find the smallest distance. The list
        points contains all points sorted by x coordinate.'''

    # If the number of points is less than or equal to 3, we can
        solve it in a trivial way.
    if num_of_points <= 3:
        return brute_force(points, num_of_points)

    # Find the middle point
    mid = num_of_points // 2
    mid_point = points[mid]

    # Compute the smallest distance
    # dl : minimum distance in the left of mid point
    # dr : minimum distance in the right side of mid point
    dl = closest_pair_recursive(points[:mid], mid)
    dr = closest_pair_recursive(points[mid:], num_of_points - mid)

    # Find the minimum of two distances
    d = min(dl, dr)

    # construct an array strip[] that contains points that are
        closer than d to mid_point
    strip = [i for i in points if abs(i[0] - mid_point[0]) < d]

    # Find the minimum distance in the points that are closer than d
        to mid_point
    strip_dis = min_strip_distance(strip, len(strip), d)

    # return the minimum from d and closest distance obtained from
        strip
    return min(d, strip_dis)
```

```
def min_strip_distance(strip, size, d):
    '''Find the distance from a strip closer than d.'''
    min_val = d

    strip.sort(key = lambda point: point[1])

    for i in range(size):
        j = i + 1
        while j < size and (strip[j][1] - strip[i][1]) < min_val:
            min_val = dist(strip[i], strip[j])
            j += 1

    return min_val

def brute_force(points, num_of_points):
    '''Calculate the smallest distance for a small number of points'
    ''
    min_val = float('inf')
    for i in range(num_of_points):
        for j in range(i + 1, num_of_points):
            if dist(points[i], points[j]) < min_val:
                min_val = dist(points[i], points[j])

    return min_val
```

In this code, we first sort the points according to their x coordinates. This would allow us to split the points into two halves efficiently. After that, we calculate the smallest distances (dl and dr) in the left and right halves recursively. The base case for the recursion is when the number of points is 3 or less, in which case we just calculate the distances between all pairs of points and return the smallest. Next, we create an array of points that are closer than 'd = min(dl, dr)' to the line passing from the middle point. Note that these points can be potential candidates for the minimum distance overall. Now, we find the smallest distance in this array and call it 'strip_dis'. The final answer would be 'min(d, strip_dis)'. The time complexity for this solution is $O(n^2)$.

This code can now be used to find the closest distance among a set of points, as explained with divide-and-conquer approach.

Chapter 12

Practical Applications of Dynamic Programming

12.1 Sequence Alignment in Bioinformatics

Sequence Alignment is a method used in bioinformatics to identify the similarities between biological sequences, such as DNA sequences or protein sequences. In this approach, two sequences are lined up and a score is assigned based on the quality of the match. The score is calculated based on some predetermined rules like what constitutes a match, mismatch, a gap etc. An algorithm for this purpose needs to be efficient since comparing sequences and aligning them can

be extremely complex due to the large size of the sequences in question. One optimal solution to sequence alignment can be achieved by using dynamic programming.

We can define sequence alignment as a problem of transforming one string into another using the least cost operations — where the operations are defined to be character insertion, deletion, or substitution. Each operation has a cost associated with it, and the alignment score is the sum of the operation costs. The problem can be solved using dynamic programming, which exploits the fact that the optimal solution to the sequence alignment problem contains within it the optimal solution to subproblems.

Here is a code snippet that demonstrates how to perform sequence alignment using dynamic programming in Python. This function creates an alignment matrix and uses it to create an optimal alignment.

```python
def sequence_alignment(seq1, seq2, match_score=1, gap_cost=2):
    # Build the alignment matrix
    alignment_matrix = [[0 for _ in range(len(seq2)+1)] for _ in
        range(len(seq1)+1)]

    for i in range(len(seq1)+1):
        alignment_matrix[i][0] = gap_cost*i
    for j in range(len(seq2)+1):
        alignment_matrix[0][j] = gap_cost*j

    # Fill the rest of the matrix
    for i in range(1, len(seq1)+1):
        for j in range(1, len(seq2)+1):
            match = alignment_matrix[i-1][j-1] + (match_score if seq1[
                i-1] == seq2[j-1] else 0)
            delete = alignment_matrix[i-1][j] + gap_cost
            insert = alignment_matrix[i][j-1] + gap_cost
            alignment_matrix[i][j] = max(match, delete, insert)

    #Reconstruct the optimal sequence
    alignment1 = ""
    alignment2 = ""
    i = len(seq1)
    j = len(seq2)
    while i > 0 or j > 0:
```

```
if i > 0 and j > 0 and alignment_matrix[i][j] ==
    alignment_matrix[i-1][j-1] + (match_score if seq1[i-1]
    == seq2[j-1] else 0):
    alignment1 = seq1[i-1] + alignment1
    alignment2 = seq2[j-1] + alignment2
    i -= 1
    j -= 1
elif i > 0 and alignment_matrix[i][j] == alignment_matrix[i
    -1][j] + gap_cost:
    alignment1 = seq1[i-1] + alignment1
    alignment2 = '-' + alignment2
    i -= 1
else:
    alignment1 = '-' + alignment1
    alignment2 = seq2[j-1] + alignment2
    j -= 1
return alignment1, alignment2
```

The complexity of this algorithm is $O(n * m)$, where n and m are the lengths of the two sequences. This is because we are filling in a matrix with n*m cells. Each cell needs to be calculated based on the cells around it, so we need to visit each cell exactly once and perform a constant number of operations for each cell. Therefore, the time complexity is $O(n * m)$. The space complexity is also $O(n * m)$ since that is the size of the matrix we are storing in memory.

12.2 Multi-Stage Graph Problem in Operations Research

The Multi-stage graph problem is a classical problem that illustrates well the concepts of Dynamic Programming. It's used in Operations Research and it's defined as follows: given a directed graph that represents a number of stages, and each stage consists of a number of nodes, we need to find the shortest path from source to destination node (the first node to the last node). The graph has an entry node and nodes are split into

stages such that all edges move from a stage to the
next one. The node at each level is connected to one
or more nodes at the next level. The problem is solved
by dynamic programming where we break the problem
into smaller subproblems which are easier to solve.

Now that we have described the problem, let's look at a Python
implementation with explanation for this problem.

```python
# Importing the infinity constant from math library
from math import inf

# Define the cost matrix
cost = [[inf, 1, 2, 5, inf, inf, inf, inf],
        [inf, inf, inf, inf, 4, 11, inf, inf],
        [inf, inf, inf, inf, 9, 5, 16, inf],
        [inf, inf, inf, inf, inf, inf, 2, inf],
        [inf, inf, inf, inf, inf, inf, inf, 18],
        [inf, inf, inf, inf, inf, inf, inf, 13],
        [inf, inf, inf, inf, inf, inf, inf, 2]]

# Define the number of stages
N = 4

# Define the distance initial array
dist = [0] * (N + 1)

# Initialize the distance array
dist[0] = 0
for i in range(1, N + 1):
    dist[i] = inf

# Dynamic programming approach to solve Multi-stage graph problem
for i in range(N - 2, -1, -1):
    for j in range(i + 1):
        dist[j] = min(cost[j][i] + dist[i + 1] for i in range(j + 1,
            N))

print(f'The shortest path cost is {dist[0]}')
```

This code first imports the infinity constant from Python's
math library which will be used to initialize the cost matrix.
The cost matrix represents the cost of moving from one node
to another. Then it defines the number of stages and initializes the distance array which will hold the minimum distance
to reach the end from each node. The minimum cost from each

node to the end is then computed using a bottom-up dynamic
programming approach. For each node from the second last to
the first, it loops over all the edges going from this node to the
next ones and updates the minimum cost. Finally, it prints out
the minimum cost to reach the end from the source which is
stored in 'dist[0]'.

The time complexity of this algorithm is $O(N^2)$ where N is the
total number of nodes in the graph. Thus, it is efficient for large
multi-stage graphs.

12.3   Text Justification Problem in Computer Graphics

The Text Justification Problem is a common problem
in computer graphics and document design. It refers
to the process of adjusting the spaces between words
in a text block so that the lines in the text are aligned
both on the left and the right side. In this problem,
we are given a sequence of words and a limit of how
many characters each line can hold. The objective is to
minimize the 'badness' of each line, which is defined as
the cube of the number of additional spaces needed to
fill up the line. We want to break the sequence of words
into lines such that the total 'badness' is minimized.
This is a common dynamic programming problem as
it involves a sequence of decisions and it exhibits both
optimal substructure and overlapping subproblems.

We can solve this problem using a bottom-up dynamic programming approach. The Python code is as follows:

```python
def justify_text(words, limit):
    # Number of words
    n = len(words)

    # Create tables to store 'badness' values and results
    inf = float('inf')
    badness = [[inf]*n for _ in range(n)]
    min_badness = [inf]*(n+1)
    result = [0]*(n+1)

    # Fill the 'badness' table
    for i in range(n):
        badness[i][i] = limit - len(words[i])
        for j in range(i+1, n):
            badness[i][j] = badness[i][j-1] - len(words[j]) - 1

    for i in range(n):
        for j in range(i, n):
            badness[i][j] **= 3 # Cube the number of spaces

    # Dynamic programming computation
    min_badness[0] = 0
    for j in range(n):
        for i in range(j+1):
            if min_badness[i] != inf and badness[i][j] != inf
                and min_badness[i] + badness[i][j] < min_badness[j+1]:
                min_badness[j+1] = min_badness[i] + badness[i][j]
                result[j+1] = i

    # Reconstruct the optimized word sequence
    lines = []
    j = n
    while j > 0:
        lines.append(words[result[j]:j])
        j = result[j]
    lines.reverse()

    return lines
```

With this code, we first initialize a 2D list 'badness' to keep track of the badness of every possible line, and two 1D lists 'min_badness' and 'result' to keep track of the minimum total badness and the corresponding solution layout respectively. Then we fill the 'badness' list by considering all possible pairs of words that could be in the same line (lines 10-14). After calculating all the badness scores, we perform a bottom-up computation of the minimum badness using a dynamic programming table (lines 17-22). Finally, we reconstruct the layout of words that result to the minimum badness and return the result. This algorithm runs in $O(n^2)$ time complexity and requires $O(n^2)$ space to store the 'badness' scores and $O(n)$ space to store the 'min_badness' and 'result' arrays.

Chapter 13

Chapter 13: Closing Thoughts

As we arrive at the concluding chapter of our journey through dynamic programming, it is important to take a moment to reflect on what we have achieved and explore the road that lies ahead. In this chapter, we take a look back at the key concepts, problems, and solutions we've encountered. We also look forward to future developments and how they might shape the landscape of dynamic programming in the years to come.

Recap and Reflection

Throughout this book, we've navigated the intricate landscape of dynamic programming, deconstructing complex problems into simpler subproblems, devising memoization strategies, and architecting bottom-up solutions. We've grappled with classic problems, such as the Knapsack problem, and the Longest Common Subsequence problem, and delved into more advanced topics, including graph problems and state transitions. Each problem served as a stepping stone, enabling us to gradually build a solid foundation in dynamic programming.

In doing so, we've not only learned a method for solving problems but also adopted a mindset for addressing complexity. By understanding the underlying principles of dynamic programming, we've gained the ability to tackle a vast array of problems that at first glance may have seemed insurmountable.

Future of Dynamic Programming

Looking to the future, the importance of dynamic programming in computer science and other disciplines is only set to increase. With the exponential growth of data in various fields such as bioinformatics, machine learning, and operations research, the demand for efficient algorithmic solutions is greater than ever.

Moreover, as computing hardware continues to evolve, so too will the techniques and approaches we use. For instance, parallel and distributed computing techniques offer exciting new avenues to explore, and these may, in time, lead to new variations on the traditional dynamic programming methodology.

Additional Resources for Learning

Continued learning and practice are key to mastering dynamic programming. Numerous resources are available online for further study. Websites like LeetCode, HackerRank, and CodeSignal offer hundreds of problems of varying difficulty, many of which involve dynamic programming. Books and online tutorials offer in-depth discussions of the theory behind dynamic programming. Universities often offer classes, both in-person and online, on algorithms and data structures, which typically include a component on dynamic programming.

Concluding Remarks

As we wrap up our exploration of dynamic programming, I hope that this book has not only equipped you with the skills to solve complex problems but also sparked an enduring curiosity about the field of algorithms and computation. Dynamic programming is a powerful tool, but it is also just one technique in the broader landscape of computer science. I encourage you to continue exploring, learning, and pushing the boundaries of what is possible. Remember, every complex problem is just a series of simpler problems waiting to be solved.

Thank you for joining me on this journey. I hope it has been as rewarding for you as it has been for me.

Printed in Great Britain
by Amazon

41275561R00050